I AM BRAVE

HELPING CHILDREN DEVELOP CONFIDENCE, SELF-BELIEF, RESILIENCE AND EMOTIONAL GROWTH THROUGH CHARACTER STRENGTHS AND POSITIVE AFFIRMATIONS.

BETH THOMPSON

SUPER CHARACTER STRENGTHS SERIES: BOOK 1

Be brave, be bold and believe in yourself.

Beth Thompson

Text and illustrations copyright © 2020 by Beth Thompson.
All rights reserved.

Reproduction of this book in any manner, in whole or in part, without written permission from the author is prohibited.

ISBN: 978-1-9164680-7-8

First Edition 2020

Plum Pudding Books

Hello, I am Luca.

I am brave.

I joined in the game.

I was worried I couldn't play.

I learnt something new.

I am brave!

I tried to climb the big old tree.

I couldn't do it, I was too afraid!

I tried and that's the most important thing.

I am brave!

I stood up to the big lion when he was mean.

I was scared it might make things worse.

I hurt my paw when I tripped and fell.

I cried all the way home.

It's much better now.

I am brave!

I felt nervous when I first met Emma.

I'd never seen an elephant before.

I made a new friend.

I am brave!

I put my paw up to answer a question.

I was worried I might get it wrong.

I tried my best.

I am brave!

I waited patiently for mom to come back.

I missed her so much.

She wasn't gone for long.

I am brave!

I didn't like the deep water.

My feet couldn't touch the floor.

I kept going.

I am brave!

I was worried about asking for help.

I couldn't do it on my own.

I was proud of myself.

I am brave!

I was scared of the storm.

The thunder was loud.

I was safe.

I am brave!

I am Luca. I am honest, kind and funny.

I am all of those things and I am so much more.

I am brave.

Yes, I am brave!

For parents, carers and teachers

To help a child find their brave, ask the following questions
and discuss key ideas with the child:

What was brave about Luca?

How do you think he felt when he needed to be brave?

How do you think he felt after he was brave?

Can you think of a time when you felt brave?

How did you feel?

Can you think of something brave you could do? Maybe something that you've never done before?

Is there anything that stops you being brave?

Is there anything that might help you be more brave?

Can you draw a picture, or stick a photograph in the space on the next page to show when you have been brave?

Please use or copy the rewards on the following pages to recognise and celebrate when you see a child demonstrate bravery!

For parents, carers and teachers

What is bravery?

Bravery is different for everyone. What feels brave to one child might not feel brave to another. It can be about sharing worries and asking for help, meeting new people or trying something new.

Bravery does not mean fearlessness. It means that we do not let our fears hold us back. Fear and bravery always go together, because, if there is no fear, then there is no need to be brave!

How can you help children find their brave?

Acknowledge the fear
Notice when the child is worried, nervous or afraid and acknowledge their fear. Let the child know that it is normal and okay to be worried or afraid, and provide reassurance.

Talk it out
Talk to the child about their fear. Simply talking together might help to reduce their fear, and will also help you to understand their worries so you can provide the right support.

Help them to express themselves
Encourage the child to express how they feel. If they can, encourage them to write it down, act it out, or draw a picture. Incorporate their fear into a game or role play situation.

Encourage them to try new things
Encourage the child to 'have a go' and try something new – a new food, a new game or visit a new place. Help them set small challenges and celebrate when they achieve them.

Prepare them for new situations or activities
Before any new situation or activity, talk to the child about what might happen. Ask them to think about how they might feel and discuss what might help them feel better.

Praise them when they show bravery
When you see a child show bravery, identify the bravery and praise them. Remember to praise their effort, commitment, enthusiasm or progress, not just the achievement.

Let them know it is okay to fail
Explain to the child that it is okay to fail and that failure is often a result of trying something brave. Every experience they have, both good and bad, will help them learn.

Show them what bravery looks like
If you want a child to be brave, show them how. Talk to them about times when you have felt nervous, anxious, or fearful, and how you managed those feelings.

My name is ....

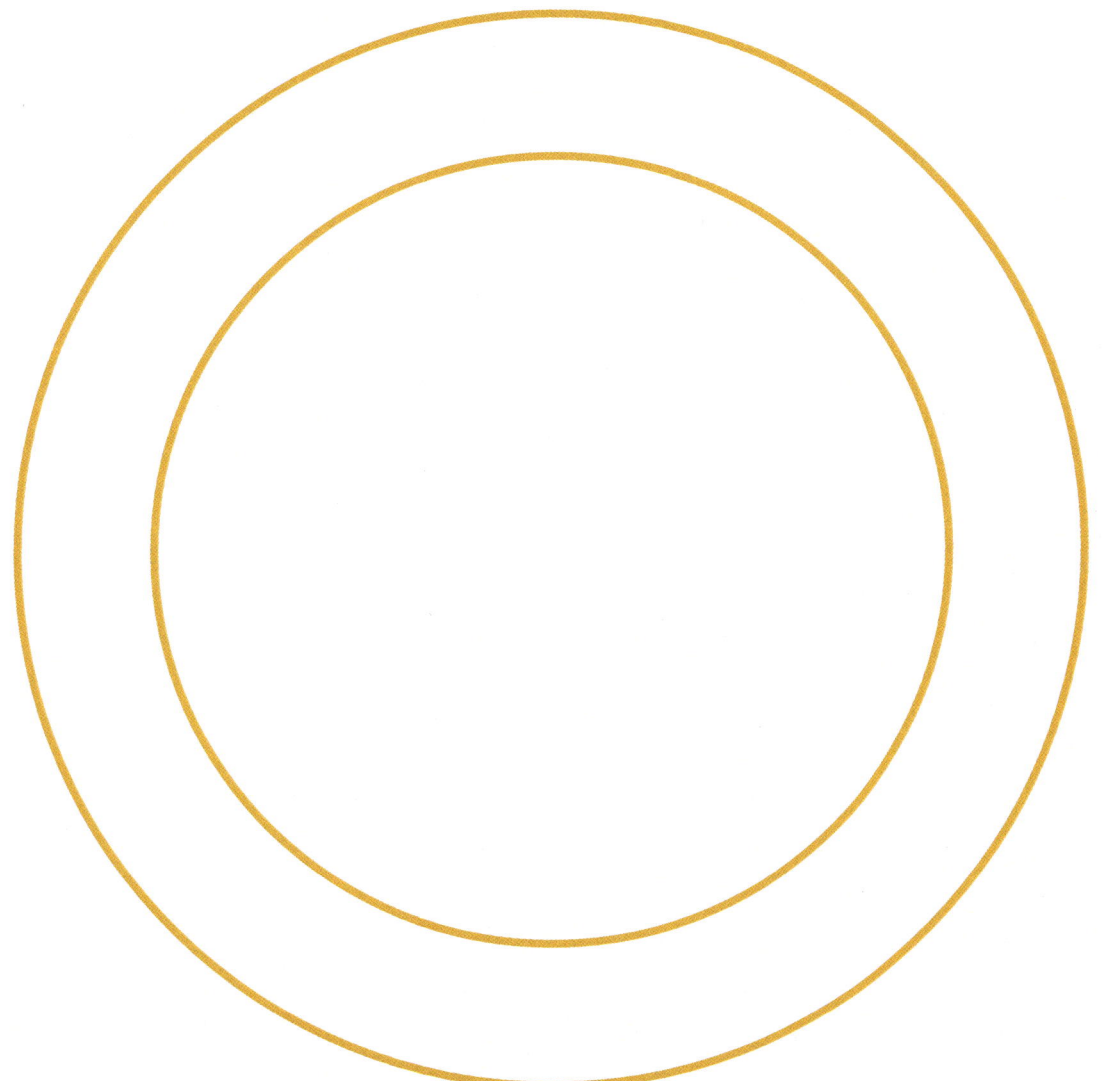

I am brave!

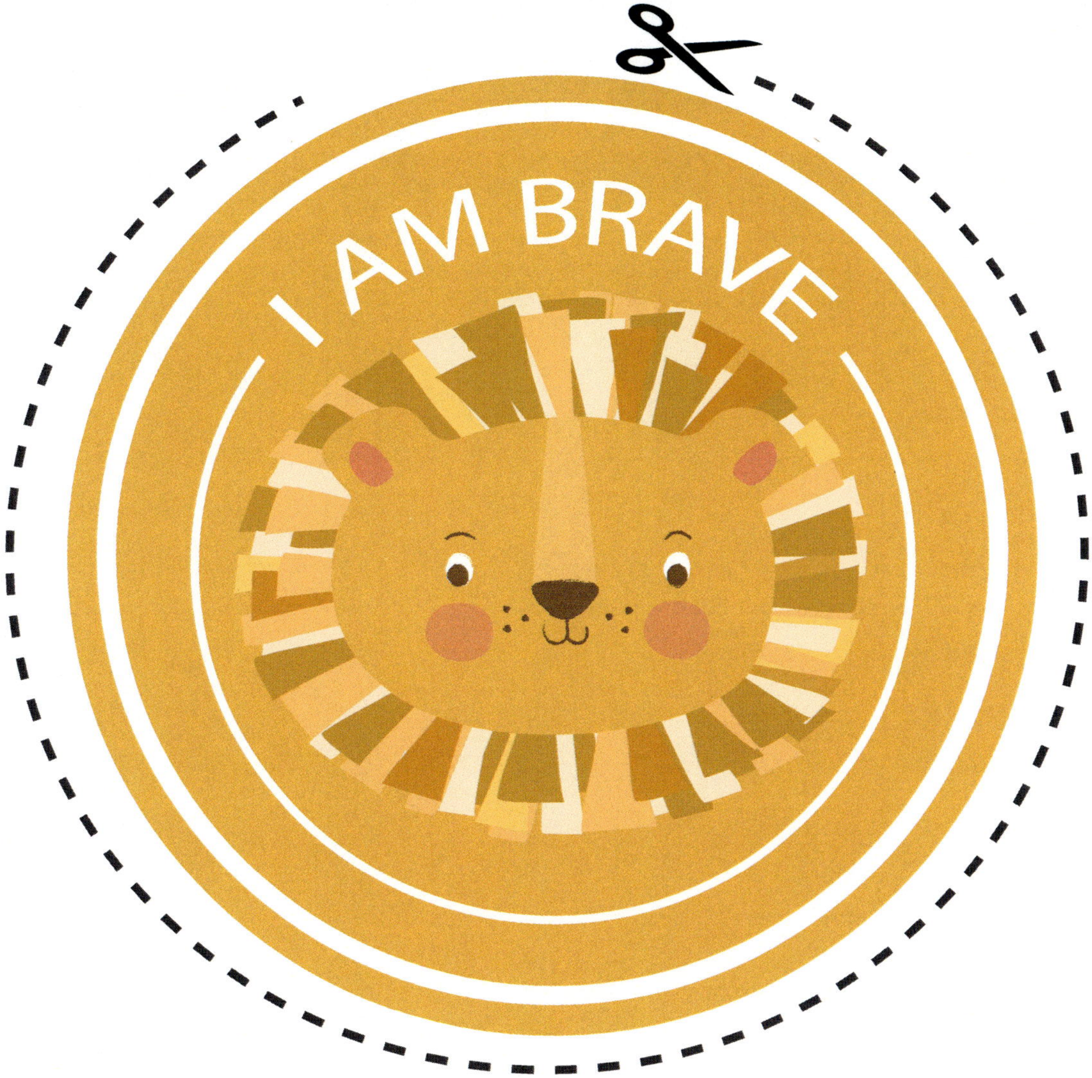
I AM BRAVE

I AM BRAVE

I AM BRAVE

I AM BRAVE

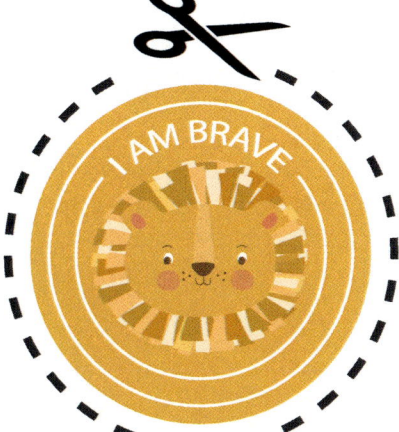

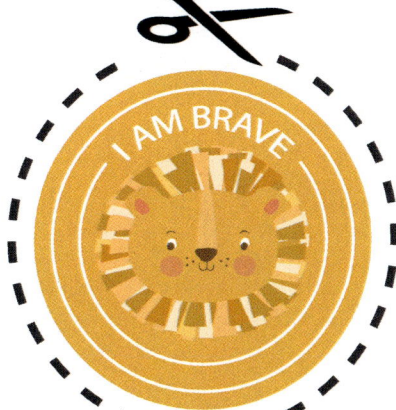

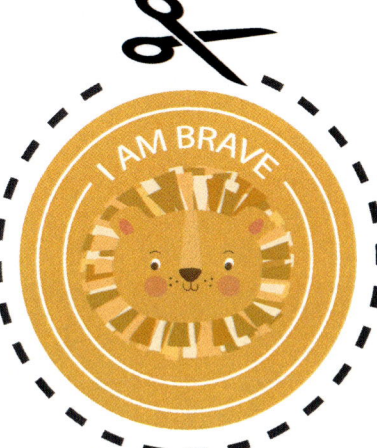

Made in the USA
Middletown, DE
11 June 2021